PLATFORM GAMES

By

Kirsty Holmes

BookLife
PUBLISHING

©2019
BookLife Publishing Ltd.
King's Lynn
Norfolk PE30 4LS
All rights reserved.
Printed in Malaysia.

A catalogue record for this book is available from the British Library.

ISBN: 978-1-78637-408-0

Written by:
Kirsty Holmes

Edited by:
Holly Duhig

Designed by:
Gareth Liddington

CONTENTS

Words that look like *this* can be accessed
in the <<GLOSSARY>> on page 31

WELCOME TO THE ARCADE

So, you want to get good at platform games, eh? Have you got ninja-like *reflexes*, super-human shooting skills and really nimble thumbs? Then fire up your joystick and get comfy: it's time to **STEP INTO THE ARCADE...**

Ever since the very first gamer got their hands on the very first video game, kids like you and me have been rushing through their homework and just waiting for Saturday to settle in front of the TV and play their favourite game. Nothing beats the thrill of beating your high score – or your older brother's! If you've picked up this book and stepped into the Arcade with us here, you've probably already played a bit – maybe you're even pretty good – but you want to find out more. This gaming guide will level up your knowledge of platform games and take you from *noob* to know-it-all in no time: so, pick up a controller and GET YOUR GAME ON!

Hey, a new player! I'm Pixelle. I LOVE gaming – do you? You do? Awesome! I expect you're here to find out more about games. Today, I'm going to see the Arcade to find out all about platformers. The Arcade is a supercomputer – it's really cool. Are you ready to enter the Arcade? Press start to begin, and let's go!

Let's start with the basics. A video game is an *electronic* game that needs a player (that's you) to use a device (that's the thing you play on) to make stuff happen on a screen. Usually, that screen is a television or a computer monitor, but you can play games on mobile phones, hand-held gaming devices or tablets too. To play on your television you will need a console – this is a special type of computer just for playing video games. If you play on a computer screen you will probably use a PC. This stands for personal computer and is a type of computer designed to be used at home by regular people for lots of things – like doing homework or using the internet – and playing games, of course! There are lots of types of video games. From *pixel*-perfect platformers and puzzlers to amazing action-adventure games that will see you virtually risking virtual life and limb, there is something in video games for everyone.

Ready to go explore the Arcade? Today, we're going to look at the games that started it all – PLATFORM GAMES!

<<Player One... Ready...?>>

ARCADE

DATA FILE: PLATFORM GAMES

Ok, gamer. We're ready to start. Arcade – load data, please.

<<LOADING... DATA LEVEL ONE: WHAT IS A PLATFORM GAME?>>

A platform game is a type of action game. The player controls a character who must travel across a series of platforms, avoiding **obstacles** and enemies, to either make it to the next level or achieve an **objective**. These can be set anywhere, but will usually show an uneven path and lots of floating platforms, and the player may need to control the character to run, jump, climb ladders, swing on ropes and avoid traps and spikes to complete the level. Levels can be realistic, or set in a cartoon, fantasy land. Often there are collectibles – items which are valuable, or useful – for the player to collect on the way, which may be worth points or give special abilities, health points or extra lives.

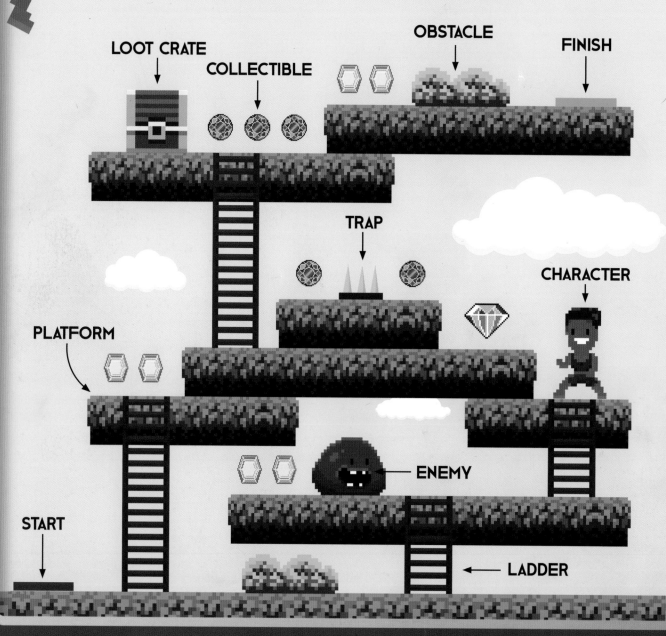

LOOT CRATE

COLLECTIBLE

OBSTACLE

FINISH

TRAP

CHARACTER

PLATFORM

ENEMY

START

LADDER

PUZZLE PLATFORMER

These games use a platformer style, but most of the gameplay takes the form of puzzles to solve.

RUN-AND-GUN

Sometimes called platform shooters, these games are all about the guns. Players have to shoot their enemies whilst running along the platforms.

CINEMATIC PLATFORMER

These games use realistic *graphics* and gameplay to create beautiful games.

ENDLESS RUNNER

The player never stops running! The levels can go on forever and the player must jump, climb and swing – but can't stop!

SIDE-SCROLLING

Games where the screen moves across sideways as the player moves through the level.

PLATFORM-ADVENTURE

These games use a platform style but include elements of adventure games too.

3D PLATFORMERS

Platform games where the player sees the action from behind the character, as if they are in game.

FACT FILE: SUPER MARIO BROS.

It's-a Maaaaario! If there's one character that stands above the rest in the game world, it's Nintendo's lovable plumber, Mario. His first appearance in a video game was in Donkey Kong, the famous *arcade* classic, except he wasn't called Mario; back then he was called Jumpman. It didn't take long for Nintendo to realise that this new hero was a star in the making and the little red plumber appeared a couple of years later in his own adventure.

From there, Mario has never looked back, starring in countless games, many of which have *defined* platform games. In Super Mario Bros., which launched on the Nintendo Entertainment System in 1985, gaming's leading man became the icon for a *generation* and the star of several side-scrolling platform greats.

In 1996, Mario once again changed the gaming world with Super Mario 64, which was one of the first games to land on the N64. In fact, Mario has featured in brilliant games for all of Nintendo's consoles including the latest, the Nintendo Switch. Super Mario Odyssey is the newest adventure in the series and some people have even gone as far as calling it the best game ever made.

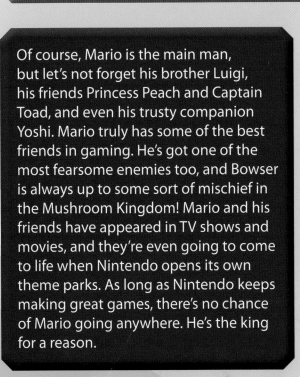

Of course, Mario is the main man, but let's not forget his brother Luigi, his friends Princess Peach and Captain Toad, and even his trusty companion Yoshi. Mario truly has some of the best friends in gaming. He's got one of the most fearsome enemies too, and Bowser is always up to some sort of mischief in the Mushroom Kingdom! Mario and his friends have appeared in TV shows and movies, and they're even going to come to life when Nintendo opens its own theme parks. As long as Nintendo keeps making great games, there's no chance of Mario going anywhere. He's the king for a reason.

TECH TALK

If you're going to be good at platform games, you need to know what you're talking about. This data file is crammed with loads of information about this type of game – let's take a look. Arcade, tell us what we need to know.

<<LOADING... DATA LEVEL THREE: WHAT YOU NEED TO KNOW>>

PLAYER INFO

Play in one-player or two-player modes, either online or on the same console with two controllers. Some games even offer play for a group of players at once! In two-player mode, the screen might split into two, or you might play on the same screen.

PERIPHERALS

Peripherals **(say: per-if-er-als)** are things you plug into the console or PC to play the game. Most platform games only need the basic controllers that come with your game. If you are playing online, you will need a headset to talk to other players. If you play on a *touchscreen* then you don't need peripherals.

VISUALS

Most platformers take place on a single path, with lots of levels and platforms the player must cross or use. Some are flat, **2D** worlds and some are **3D**. Graphics can be simple pixel images or beautiful artworks. Levels can take place on a single, fixed screen or a side-scrolling landscape.

CONTROLS

The most important control in any platformer is the JUMP button. Jumping gets you from level to level. In some games, your only attack is jumping on enemies so practise this a lot! Next up is FIRE, which is handy for taking out enemies with a fireball or two. More advanced controls include swinging, climbing or bouncing on trampolines.

LEVELS

Most games will offer a **tutorial** level to help you learn the controls. The first levels will usually be quite easy, and as you progress to higher levels, the game will slowly become harder. This is called a learning curve. If games didn't get harder, you'd soon get bored! The hardest levels are called boss levels. Here, you meet a very tough enemy and must defeat them to progress.

FACT FILE:

Sega's blue hedgehog is one of the most famous characters in the gaming world. Even if you've never run a loop-de-loop in his shoes, you've probably watched him on the television or seen his face in a magazine. Sonic became a household name thanks to his fast feet and funky attitude, and it certainly helps that he's got one of the catchiest theme tunes around!

Sonic became such a huge star in the gaming world that he started appearing in all sorts of different types of games and, so far, he's starred in his own Olympic games alongside Mario, and in racing games, pinball games, and even 3D action-adventures. Sonic is still a popular character and it doesn't look like he's going to slow down anytime soon.

Sonic started life as a platform hero, running through levels at super speeds, grabbing all of the gold rings that he can, spinning into his enemies, avoiding dangerous spikes, and eventually squaring off against Doctor Robotnik – also known as Doctor Eggman – in challenging boss battles. Sonic might have jumped on the heads of his enemies, but in the end, he was saving the local wildlife that had been transformed by the evil Doctor.

When Sonic wasn't jumping on platforms and dodging enemies, he was looking for secrets hidden throughout the levels. On top of the gold coins found all over the place, there were power-ups that gave Sonic a shield, made him *invincible* or made him run even faster!

Sonic started off on his own but when it came to the second game in the series he was joined by his trusty friend, Miles 'Tails' Prower, who was the first in a growing cast of characters that would join the lightning-quick hedgehog in future adventures, including Amy Rose and Knuckles the Echidna **(say: eh-KID-na)**.

TIMELINE OF PLATFORM GAMES

> Time for a history lesson. We'll need to access the archives for this one. Arcade, please access and display timeline files.

START

`<<LOADING... DATA LEVEL FOUR: PLATFORM GAMES TIMELINE>>`

EARLY 1980S

Although other games, like Space Panic and Crazy Climber existed, most people think the first true platform game was Nintendo's Donkey Kong, released in 1981 in arcades. In 1983 Mario Bros. was released. Most of these games had a fixed screen, and the goal was to climb the platforms to the top.

LATE 1980S

Side-scrolling gameplay started to become popular with the release of Super Mario Bros. This game became the leader of the *genre* with many similar games coming out soon after. Handheld consoles, such as the Nintendo Game Boy and Sega Game Gear, put platforming in people's pockets.

EARLY 1990S

Better technology in consoles led to more complex games. Sonic the Hedgehog was released in 1990 by Sega, rocketing platformers into the 90s with breakneck speed. Games like Prince of Persia pushed the limits of animation and appealed to older players too.

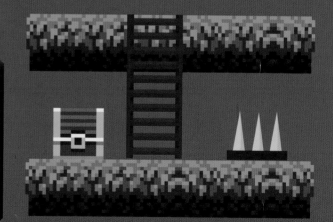

RIGHT NOW

There has been a renewed interest in platform games into the 2010s and beyond. Mobile gaming has provided a new platform for these games, and we are seeing new ways of playing them. Games like Sony's LittleBigPlanet have mixed platform gaming with world-building, and the big characters are still going strong.

THE 21ST CENTURY

As consoles developed and games became more complicated, platform games slowly stopped being the most popular games around. Big games like Rayman and Sonic continued, but many big-name games started moving away from the platform experience.

LATE 1990S

2D platformers were still popular, with titles like Rayman and Oddworld leading the genre. Games like Crash Bandicoot and Spyro the Dragon brought 3D graphics and gameplay to platform games.

FACT FILE: RUNNER 3

Not all games are made by studios with dozens – sometimes hundreds – of people, and there are lots of smaller studios out there making great games. You've probably played some on a mobile device or even on websites with your parents. These smaller teams of developers are often referred to as indies, and one such indie studio is Choice Provisions.

The studio made its name by making a number of similar-looking games in what they called the Bit.Trip series, and one of the games in that series was called Bit.Trip Runner. The game had *pixel graphics* and starred a quirky little character by the name of CommanderVideo.

The studio expanded on the idea with cute 3D graphics in the brilliantly-named Bit.Trip Presents... Runner2: Future Legend of Rhythm Alien, which saw the return of CommanderVideo, this time sprinting through colourful worlds. In 2018, he returned in Runner3 – this time with a number of friends to keep him company and some new *gameplay mechanics*.

The action in Runner3 is fast and frantic, and the player has to react quickly to every obstacle that appears in their path by quickly swapping between sliding and jumping at exactly the right second. It's tough, and sometimes you have to be able to try it again and again until you reach the end of the level. It's certainly not a good game for anyone who gets upset when they get stuck!

GET YOUR GAME ON

OK, so it's time to play. Load up your chosen platformer, stretch out those thumbs, and get comfy. Arcade: please load the gaming guide.

<<LOADING... DATA LEVEL FIVE: HOW TO PLAY>>

PRESS START TO BEGIN

If you're new to platforming, pick a game and play the tutorial carefully to learn the controls you need to play. If you have more experience, see if your game has difficulty settings – ranging from EASY to IMPOSSIBLE, a game can feel totally different on a harder setting.

OBJECTIVES

The aim of the game is known as your objective. This will be different from game to game, so make sure you know what you're trying to achieve. Maybe you have to complete the level as fast as possible. Perhaps there's someone in distress to rescue, or you have to find all the collectibles before you can leave. Knowing this will help you plan your *strategy*.

YOU LOST A LIFE

Platform games often require trial-and-error – this means that you will probably die a lot of times in the game before you can complete a level. Make sure you save your game whenever you can. Some games will give you a certain amount of 'lives' – a set number of times you can receive a *fatal* injury before it's GAME OVER. Others will have a health bar – this will decrease as you are injured until it's empty and GAME OVER. Some games have permadeath – this means that when you're dead, it's GAME OVER. Find out which collectible gives you an 'extra life' and collect as many of these as you can, otherwise – you guessed it – GAME OVER!

PATTERN POWER

Platform games are all about patterns. Look for the timing of an enemy movement – often, an enemy will move back and forth across a small area in a repeating pattern – knowing this pattern is key to getting past it. But enemies aren't your only problem when jumping through your level. In a platform game, you are more likely to die from a mistimed jump with you landing impaled in a pit of spikes or plummeting to your death in a bottomless pit.

<<KILLER BYTES>>
PRACTISE, PRACTISE, PRACTISE; THE MORE YOU PLAY AND LEARN THE PATTERNS, THE BETTER YOU WILL BE AT THE GAME

FACT FILE: LittleBIG Planet 3

If you've got a PlayStation at home, or even if you've played on one at a friend's house, the chances are that you've come across LittleBigPlanet. Even if you haven't, you probably still know about their mascot, Sackboy, and his fabulous fabric friends.

The LittleBigPlanet games are creative platformers filled with puzzles for players to overcome using Sackboy and his ingenious abilities. The main *campaign* sees you play as Sackboy – and you can collect and customise his fabric skin, clothing, hats and shoes – even fun costumes! Running and jumping make up most of his moves, but you also have a secret weapon: the Popit menu. This menu contains everything Sackboy needs to get around his world, including new gadgets you find on your travels, and fun stickers to decorate your own little world.

Over the years, the LittleBigPlanet universe has spilled over into kart racing, and there's even a game called PlayStation All-Stars that puts famous characters in the ring together. Sackboy's most recent appearance was in LittleBigPlanet 3 which included co-op play for up to four friends to play together.

Sackboy might be best known as a platform hero, but there's something else that makes the LittleBigPlanet series special, and that's the freedom it gives the player. You can use a really powerful set of tools to create your own levels. In the more recent entries in the series, the tools became really clever, including portals, trampolines and the ability to build, share and play your own levels from scratch, and if you work really hard to learn how it works you can even create your own games!

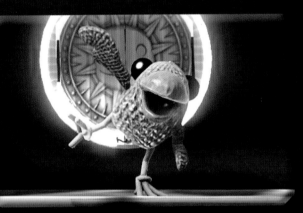

CONSOLE PROFILE

While most consoles can play all types of games, there is one company whose consoles have been linked to platform games since the very beginning: Nintendo. Let's take a look at the machines behind Mario and find out more…

1977: COLOUR TV-GAME

Data: Small console with up to six games. Only released in Japan. 5 versions. 1-2 Players.

1980: GAME & WATCH

Data: Handheld console. 1 game installed. Features: clock and alarm.

1983: (NES) NINTENDO ENTERTAINMENT SYSTEM

Data: 8-*bit* TV console. First worldwide release. Sold: 61.9 million. Games on large cartridges. Known as Famicom in Japan. Launched huge games such as Donkey Kong and The Legend of Zelda.

Nintendo®

2017: NINTENDO SWITCH

Data: *Hybrid* console: with television when 'docked', as a screen and controller when on a table, and as a handheld gaming tablet when the controllers are attached. Controllers known as joy-cons use movement and buttons. Games: The Legend of Zelda; Breath of the Wilds.

2012: NINTENDO WII U

Data: A small console and tablet-like GamePad device meant that users could play on the TV, or on the handheld device's screen – or even both at once!

2006: NINTENDO WII

Data: Wii Remotes control games through movement and buttons. Other peripherals included a steering wheel, nunchucks, tennis rackets and guns.

1989: GAME BOY

Data: First handheld console with cartridges, and many games. Over 100 million sold. Later versions include Game Boy Light and Game Boy Colour, with colour graphics.

1990: SUPER NINTENDO ENTERTAINMENT SYSTEM

Data: 16-bit TV console. Best-selling console of the 16-bit *era* of video games – 49.1 million sold. Upgraded some popular games and released new ones, including Super Mario Bros.

1995: (N64) NINTENDO 64

Data: 64-bit TV console. Games: GoldenEye 007, The Legend of Zelda: The Ocarina of Time.

1995: NINTENDO GAMECUBE

Data: Games on disks. Games: Super Mario Sunshine, Metroid Prime, Animal Crossing and Pikmin.

2004: NINTENDO DS

Data: Handheld console with two screens and a *stylus*. Other versions: 3DS (3D screens), 2DS

FACT FILE: STARBOUND

You've fled your home, only to discover you're lost in space! Your only hope is to beam yourself down from your damaged ship, and hope the world below can provide everything you need to get back into the vast, infinite universe…

While not strictly speaking a platform game, exploration-based game Starbound is an action-adventure game that shares a lot with the platform genre – and breaks a lot of the rules too. Starbound is a 2D world that players can freely explore; and unlike many platform games, allows you to create your own story. Will you choose to save the universe – or become its ruler, colonising planets and mining their resources? Maybe you'll spend your time farming the land, or rake in the virtual cash as an intergalactic landlord, renting out space to the highest bidder. The choice is yours.

Starbound really breaks the mould of this kind of game; with thousands of objects and hundreds of materials, you can mine, farm and build, just like in a world-building game such as Minecraft, and you can freely explore the world; this game may look like a platform game but it's a groundbreaker (and we don't just mean the miners here).

And you aren't alone on this alien world, either. Multiplayer options mean you can play with friends or strangers – it's a whole community of people lost in the galaxy, just trying to make an honest living (and deal with the penguins). The world is enormous – it's procedurally-generated. This means that each new screen or area is created anew by the program itself, so you really are exploring new terrain with each game. This allows the game to be both deceptively simple and amazingly complex. With this big little game from Chucklefish studios, you really are going where no pixelated person has gone before.

PRO TALK

Let's find out more about games by talking to some professionals. Gaming professionals are people who do something in gaming to earn a living, such as making videogames or writing about them in magazines. These pros really know their stuff – so let's hear their advice and tips.

DANT RAMBO

Writer and producer at Choice Provisions. When he's not working on the *narrative* for a game, he's making sure everyone on the team gets their work done on time. It's a pretty good life.

1. WHAT MAKES GAMES FUN TO PLAY WITH YOUR FRIENDS?

"We really tend to lean towards multiplayer games that make us laugh. Games like Overcooked, WarioWare, and Mario Kart come to mind, because they're all games you can have fun with whether you win or lose. The fun is baked right into the formula, making them sure-fire bets when looking for a game to play with your friends."

2. WHY DO WE LIKE CHALLENGING AND DIFFICULT GAMES?

"Accomplishing something challenging is always a great feeling, and with games in particular, it's easy to see yourself improve as you play. Struggling with a boss? Chances are you'll do a little bit better each time you fight it. You continue to improve as you continue to play, until finally you manage to pull it off."

3. WHAT MAKES A GREAT VIDEO GAME CHARACTER?

"A character that helps the player connect to the game they're playing. Even if the character is silly, evil, or completely silent, you want the player to connect with them in some way. Of course, it always helps if the player sees a little of themselves in the character they're playing as. This is why *representation* in games is so important."

4. WHAT CAN GAMES DO THAT OTHER MEDIUMS CAN'T?

"The interactive nature of games allows them to affect people in ways other mediums aren't able to. A video game has the opportunity to not only ask the player a question, but allow them the chance to answer it. Video games let you be a part of the story, and to see an outcome based on your own actions can make for a great lesson in *empathy*."

5. HOW CAN GAMES HELP US BE MORE CREATIVE?

"I personally think most games have the ability to encourage creativity. This is especially true in modern games, which more often than not provide the player with several different options as to how they want to make their way through the game. This encourages creative decision-making, which is a skill that is very important in the real world!"

6. HOW DO YOU BALANCE SIMULATION WITH FUN?

"That's a tricky question! For us, our focus with every game we release is on making it as fun as possible. Most of us on the team like silly, unrealistic games, which in turn inspires us to make silly games of our own. Everyone's idea of fun is different, so it comes down to a matter of taste. For us, however, we strive to make the funnest, goofiest games we possibly can."

WORK AND PLAY

Do you like playing video games? When you grow up, wouldn't that be a cool job? Did you know that you can actually work on video games? Yes, that's right – people will pay you to play games! But that's not all. There are loads of jobs in gaming, and it's more than just playing games. Let's find out more...

THE JOB SHOP

EXTRA! EXTRA!

The video games industry is so large that it has its own journalists. Journalists are people who know a LOT about video games and write about them in newspapers, magazines and websites. They get to meet people who work in gaming, interview them, and write about them afterwards. If you like games, and writing, then this could be the job for you!

GOOD INFLUENCE

Some people, called influencers, play and talk about video games online, on streaming sites such as YouTube and Twitch. They get paid for this through sponsorships and advertising.

GET WITH THE PROGRAM

Programmers write the code that makes the game work. They use different computer languages to tell the game what to do. If you like maths, computers and coding, you'll love getting paid to do this!

ONCE UPON A TIME

Narrative designers write stories, characters and levels for games. Big games such as Skyrim or Mass Effect have lots of narrative designers working together, while smaller games might only have one! If you like stories, this could be a great job for you.

WORK OF ART

Graphics designers create the visuals for a game. They draw the scenery, characters and maps for games and give them a distinctive style. If you like drawing, painting and art, as well as games, you'd love this job.

QUALITY STREET

Once a game is made, someone has to check it's all working properly. Playtesters play games in the early stages to look for problems, difficulty, and story problems. If you like playing games and you're very, very thorough, you'll enjoy this job.

IN PUBLIC

People in public relations (PR) tell the public, and journalists, about the games they represent. They create interesting adverts, talk to the press, and tell everyone how brilliant their games are. If you're friendly, chatty and social, and a bit creative, you'll love working in PR.

CONTINUE?

You made it to the end! Well done. We can leave the Arcade now if you want to, and go play some amazing platform games. Or, if you're not finished learning, you can go to these websites to find out more...

<<CONTINUE? Y/N>>
HTTP://PLAYSTARBOUND.COM/

<<CONTINUE? Y/N>>
WWW.SEGA.CO.UK

<<CONTINUE? Y/N>>
HTTPS://WWW.PLAYSTATION.COM/EN-GB/GAMES/LITTLEBIGPLANET-3-PS4/

<<CONTINUE? Y/N>>
HTTPS://WWW.RUNNER3.GAME/

GLOSSARY

2D — two-dimensional – an item with width and height

3D — three-dimensional – an item with width, depth and height

arcade — purpose-built public place dedicated to video games, usually in coin-operated cabinets

bit — the smallest unit of information in a computer

campaign — the events that create the main action or storyline in a video game

defined — something that is clear, and represents something else well

electronic — using electricity to function

empathy — identifying with or sharing the feelings of someone else

era — a set period of time

fatal — causing death

gameplay mechanics — the rules and methods of a video game; how players interact with a game

generation — groups of things or people that are roughly the same age

genre — a particular type or sort of something

graphics — images on a computer screen

hybrid — when two different things are combined to make something new

invincible — cannot be defeated

narrative — the storyline or sequence of actions in a game

noob — someone who is new and inexperienced, especially in the world of video games

objective — something you are trying to achieve

obstacles — things that get in the way and must be overcome

pixel — tiny dots of light that make up the images on a screen

pixel graphics — simple graphics made of squares displayed on a video game screen

reflexes — responses that are automatic and not controlled by conscious thought

representation — when people of different social groups (e.g. ethnicities) are visibly present in the media

strategy — a plan, or series of actions, that will achieve a desired outcome

stylus — a writing instrument for use with screens or video games

touchscreen — a computer screen that can be used by touching with the fingertips or a stylus

tutorial — a teaching level in which gamers learn the controls for a particular game

<<SAVING KNOWLEDGE. DO NOT SHUT DOWN. SYSTEMS SHOW ALL DATA SAVED IN MEMORY BANK. WELL DONE.>>

INDEX

<<THANKS FOR ACCESSING THE ARCADE TODAY. WE HOPE YOU HAD THE BEST TIME. SHUTTING DOWN IN 3... 2... 1...>>